CONTENTS

Some words are shown in the text in bold, **like this**. You can find out what they mean by looking in the glossary on page 31.

THE WORLD CUP

The **FIFA** World Cup is the most important football **tournament** in the world. The first World Cup was held in 1930, in Uruguay, South America. Uruguay was chosen as the **host** because its team was the current Olympic football champion. Most of the teams that participated were from Central and South America. The United States also came.

The World Cup in Uruguay was difficult for the European teams because travelling long distances was much more difficult in 1930 than it is today. The teams would not have travelled by plane. They would have had to go on a long and tiring sea journey from Europe to South America. Uruguay beat their South American neighbours Argentina in the first ever World Cup final on 30 July 1930. They won the match 4–2.

World Cup 2010

The 2010 FIFA World Cup will be held in South Africa. It will be the first time that the tournament has been held on the African **continent**. The number of teams taking part in the World Cup has more than doubled since the first tournament. There will be 32 teams competing in South Africa in 2010 compared to 13 in Uruguay in 1930.

Italy won the 2006 World Cup. They beat France in the final.

Today, teams are not invited to play. They have to qualify for the right to be involved in the most important football tournament in the world. The only team that does not have to qualify is the team of the host nation.

Goals galore

Both of the World Cup semi-final matches in 1930 ended with the same incredible score line: 6–1. Argentina beat USA, and Uruguay beat Yugoslavia.

GREAT MATCHES

Since the **FIFA** World Cup began, many great matches have been played. Some of these matches have involved great individual performances or **controversial** incidents. The greatest matches are often the semi-finals and finals, because there is so much at stake!

England vs West Germany 1966

The 1966 World Cup was held in England. It was the first time that England had **hosted** the world's most important football **tournament**, and the players and the public were very excited.

England lined up in red shirts on the day of the final. They were slight favourites over West Germany who wore their traditional white and black colours. It was a close match that ended 2–2 in normal time, after Germany equalized in the 89th minute! The England players showed great strength physically and mentally to keep playing well in **extra time**. Alan Ball, the England **midfielder**, was inspirational to his teammates, and England again started to look like favourites for the title.

Stolen!

In the build-up to the final the Jules Rimet trophy was stolen. It was found by a dog out walking with his owner in a London park. The dog, named Pickles, became an instant hero with the English public.

Controversial goal

England scored a controversial goal in extra time to make the score 3–2. Geoff Hurst, who had equalled the score at 1–1 earlier in the game, managed to hit a shot past the West German goalkeeper. His shot hit the crossbar and bounced down. England's players immediately began celebrating a goal as the referee and linesman discussed whether the goal should stand. They decided that the ball had crossed the goal line: it was a goal.

STATS

TEAMS: ENGLAND, WEST GERMANY

DATE: 30TH JULY 1966

VENUE: WEMBLEY STADIUM, LONDON

ATTENDANCE: 93,000

FINAL SCORE: 2–2, AET 4–2

England, the huge Wembley crowd behind them, knew that they just needed to keep the score as it was to be world champions. In the closing seconds of the game, England's captain Bobby Moore played a long ball out from defence. Geoff Hurst latched on to the ball, ran past the West German defence, and took a shot. It was a goal, a hat-trick for Hurst. The score was 4–2, the match was over, and England had won the World Cup final.

Italy vs Brazil 1970

The 1970 **FIFA** World Cup final has been described by many as the greatest ever football match. One reason for this was a clash of playing styles. The Brazil team was full of skill and flair. The Italians were strong, solid, and reliable.

The majority of fans in the stadium wanted Brazil to win. Everyone liked the way that they played football: with quick, **incisive** passing and **midfielders** with speed and brilliant **dribbling** skills. Added to this, of course, they had football **legend** Pelé. This was to be his last World Cup appearance and many fans wanted to see him lift the trophy for the third time in his career.

STATS

TEAMS: BRAZIL, ITALY

DATE: 21ST JUNE 1970

VENUE: AZTECA STADIUM, MEXICO CITY, MEXICO

ATTENDANCE: 107, 412

FINAL SCORE: 4–1

At the time of the 1970 World Cup, Pelé was the greatest footballer in the world.

In the World Cup final, Italy could not match the amazing football skills of the Brazil team.

Brazilian magic

Brazil started the match slightly better than the Italians. They had a few chances to score before Pelé put them 1–0 ahead in the 18th minute. This early goal seemed to make Brazil relax too much. Italy managed to get through the Brazilian defence and score. At half-time the score was level at 1–1.

Colour TV

The 1970 World Cup final was the first to be shown on television in colour.

In the second half, both teams tried to control the match, but it was the individual talents of the Brazilian players that made the difference. The Brazil midfielder Gerson scored following a neat passing move involving four different players. Brazil had the advantage, 2–1. Five minutes later a cross was headed by Pelé into the path of Jairzinho. He managed to squeeze his shot past the Italian goalkeeper, 3–1.

Brazil had victory in their sights, but there were still several minutes left to play. Brazil's players began to really enjoy themselves. They passed the ball effortlessly around. Brazil scored again! Carlos Alberto received the ball from Pelé and without breaking stride he struck his shot powerfully into the goal. Brazil had won the World Cup.

West Germany vs France 1982

The 1982 semi-final between West Germany and France was a fascinating match between two of the giants of European football. France had the edge in terms of **technique**. In Michel Platini and Alain Giresse they had players who could win a match with one skilful pass or move. West Germany, in contrast, were well organized and determined. This was perhaps France's best chance to win the World Cup so far. Although West Germany had been successful in previous **tournaments**, the French were expected to win here.

STATS

TEAMS: WEST GERMANY, FRANCE

DATE: 8TH JULY 1982

VENUE: SANCHEZ PIZJUAN STADIUM, SEVILLE, SPAIN

ATTENDANCE: 70,000

FINAL SCORE: 3–3 AET, 5–4 PENS.

Early in the match France were frustrated by the Germans' defensive **tactics**. The German **defenders** and **midfielders** made it hard for France to score. West Germany scored the opening goal of the match against the run of play. Platini then levelled the score from a **penalty** to make it 1–1 at half-time.

Michel Platini (in blue) plays at the 1982 World Cup semi-final vs West Germany.

Shocking decision

Early in the second half West Germany's goalkeeper, Toni Schumacher, came rushing out of his area to tackle one of France's players. The Frenchman, Patrick Battiston, clashed with the goalkeeper and was left on the ground, unconscious. The French players and fans were horrified that the referee did not send off Schumacher. No more goals were scored in the second half, so the game went to **extra time**.

This photograph was taken just before the shocking collision between Toni Schumacher (right) and Patrick Battiston. As you can see in this photo, the ball had gone past the goalkeeper.

Both teams knew that a **penalty shoot-out** awaited them if they could not win the match in extra time. After scoring two goals in the first half of extra-time France looked as though they would go on to the final. West Germany, however, were very determined and managed to score another 2 goals to make the score 3–3. This meant a penalty shoot-out was needed.

West Germany won the shoot-out 5–4. Their goalkeeper, Schumacher, saved two of the French penalties. France were devastated. After being 3–1 up in extra time they had lost. West Germany had fought hard to make it to the final.

SHOCK RESULTS

As well as great matches, the **FIFA** World Cup has also seen some shocking results. The most shocking results are often when an **inferior** team beats a well-established football nation.

Brazil vs Uruguay 1950

Brazil were the favourites in the final of the 1950 World Cup. They were considered to be the greatest team in the world at the time. They had scored thirteen goals in their previous two matches at the World Cup and were playing on home soil. Over 170,000 people packed into the Maracana stadium to watch their team play Uruguay. Millions of people were at home listening to the match on the radio and preparing to celebrate after the final whistle.

STATS

TEAMS: BRAZIL, URUGUAY

DATE: 16TH JULY 1950

VENUE: MARACANA STADIUM, RIO DE JANEIRO, BRAZIL

ATTENDANCE: 174,000

FINAL SCORE: 1–2

Uruguay beat Brazil in front of packed crowds at the Maracana stadium in July 1950.

Uruguay had other ideas. Although they were not as good as Brazil, they certainly deserved their place in the final. Brazil took the lead at the beginning of the second half, but couldn't increase on this advantage. When Uruguay equalized the stadium fell silent. When they scored again it felt as though the whole of Brazil went quiet. Shocked, the Brazilians failed to get back into the match and Uruguay became world champions.

North Korea vs Italy 1966

Perhaps one of the biggest World Cup shocks was when North Korea knocked Italy out of the World Cup in 1966. They beat Italy 1–0. North Korea had never played in a World Cup before. Italy, one of the pre-**tournament** favourites, had to beat North Korea to go on to the second round. They were expected to win comfortably. The North Koreans had nothing to lose. After scoring before half-time they managed to hold out for a famous victory that embarrassed the Italians.

STATS

TEAMS: NORTH KOREA, ITALY

DATE: 19TH JULY 1966

VENUE: AYRESOME PARK, MIDDLESBROUGH, ENGLAND

ATTENDANCE: 20,000

FINAL SCORE: 1–0

The winning goal! This shot that went past goalkeeper Enrico Albertosi sent Italy out of the 1966 World Cup.

West Germany vs Algeria 1982

In 1982, Algeria were featuring in their first World Cup. West Germany, winners in 1974, were one of the favourites for the 1982 **tournament** held in Spain. After a goalless first half, Algeria took the lead in the 54th minute. The Germans had underestimated the Algerians and now needed to play much better to win the game. Karl-Heinz Rummenigge, one of the most famous German players, managed to score a goal. Within a minute Algeria had shocked their **opponents** again by scoring to make the score 2–1. Algeria held out for a brilliant victory.

World Cup runners up

Luckily for West Germany they managed to recover from the shocking result against Algeria. They made it all the way to the final, where they were beaten by Italy.

The Algerian players were overjoyed to beat West Germany.

Cameroon teammates piled on top of Omam Biyick in celebration, after his goal against Argentina.

Argentina vs Cameroon 1990

The opening match of each World Cup often involves the winner of the previous tournament. Argentina won the World Cup in 1986 and so played Cameroon in the opening match of the 1990 World Cup in Italy. Because they had won the last World Cup, Argentina were one of the favourites to win in 1990. Cameroon had never won a World Cup match before, drawing all three matches in their previous World Cup appearance.

STATS

TEAMS: ARGENTINA, CAMEROON

DATE: 8TH JUNE, 1990

VENUE: STADIO GIUSEPPE MEAZZA SAN SIRO, MILAN, ITALY

ATTENDANCE: 73,780

FINAL SCORE: 0–1

When Cameroon took the lead mid-way through the second half it looked like there was going to be a major shock. Despite having two players sent off, Cameroon had the determination to hold off Argentina's attacks. Cameroon had achieved the best result in their history with a 1–0 win.

USA vs Iran 1998

USA and Iran were not favourites to win the World Cup in 1998. However, USA were expected to be able to beat Iran in this group game and proceed to the next round. Iran had not won a match in their previous World Cup appearance in 1978. Most **spectators** did not think they had much of a chance against the USA.

The Iran players worked harder on the pitch and took a two-goal lead. USA scored a consolation goal in the final few minutes. Iran won the match 2–1. This result made headlines all around the world.

Before the match, most people thought that the USA would easily beat Iran.

Trouble off the pitch

Because of **political tension** between the two nations, this **FIFA** World Cup match had more significance than usual. The winners would be able to use the result to show that they had superiority over the other, at least on the football pitch.

France vs Senegal 2002

This match between France and Senegal was the opening match of the 2002 World Cup. France had won the **tournament** on home soil in 1998 and were expected to do well again. This was Senegal's first ever match in a World Cup. Most spectators expected an easy win for France. They thought the Senegal team had some promising young players, but that France had more experience.

The Senegal team had to play without fear if they were to stand a chance of winning, and they did this superbly. Although France had more **possession** and more shots, it was Senegal who managed to score. They held on for an amazing result. France did not recover from this result and failed to make it to the second round of the World Cup. The confidence gained from this result helped the Senegal team to play well in the tournament. They made it all the way to the quarter-finals.

The France players (in blue) were devastated and humiliated after they were beaten by Senegal.

GREAT GOALS

S ince the **FIFA** World Cup began in 1930 there have been 2,063 goals scored in the 18 **tournaments** up to 2006. Whether the goals come from **free kicks**, **penalties**, own goals, headers, long range, or tap-ins, they all count. Some of the goals scored have been spectacular.

Esteban Cambiasso (Argentina) vs Serbia & Montenegro 2006

This goal is considered by many fans to be the greatest goal since Carlos Alberto's goal for Brazil in 1970 (see page 21). The standard of play in the World Cup is usually very high. **Possession** of the ball is very important. During this group game, Argentina taught their **opponents** a lesson about keeping possession of the ball.

The ball was passed between teammates more than 20 times before it reached Cambiasso. He traded passes with Hernan Crespo just inside the 18-yard box. Cambiasso was left with the task of putting the ball into the goal. He placed his shot to the left of the goalkeeper, into the net. It was a fantastic goal.

Cambiasso's shot flew past the goalkeeper to finish off a great move by Argentina.

This photo was taken just before Michael Owen scored his amazing World Cup goal.

Michael Owen (England) vs Argentina 1998

Playing in his first World Cup, Michael Owen was only 18 when he scored this great goal. David Beckham played a simple **through-ball** to Owen just inside the Argentina half. He used his pace and agility to glide past a couple of Argentina **defenders**. Then he smashed his shot past the goalkeeper from just inside the penalty area. From this point on, everyone knew who Michael Owen was. He had announced his football talent to the world.

Using his pace and skill, Maradona dribbled the ball past several England players, before scoring his incredible goal.

Diego Maradona (Argentina) vs England 1986

One of the greatest goals ever scored in a World Cup **tournament** was in the 1986 match between Argentina and England. Diego Maradona scored both his team's goals when they beat England 2–1.

Although there was **controversy** about Maradona's first goal, the second one was simply brilliant. He received the ball inside the Argentina half and quickly got past two English players. Using his natural balance and skill with the ball he began to move into the England half. With a burst of pace he **dribbled** the ball past two England **defenders**, and into the England **penalty** area.

After taking the ball past five players, Maradona then took the ball past the English goalkeeper. When another desperate tackle came in, he used his strength to hold off the challenge. He slotted the ball into the net. It was an amazing goal and an incredible achievement!

Carlos Alberto (Brazil) vs Italy 1970

The last goal in the final of the 1970 World Cup is regarded by many fans as the greatest goal ever scored in World Cup history. Brazil were already beating Italy 3–1 and the Italians appeared to have accepted defeat. With five minutes left to go it looked as though Brazil were going to play it safe and keep **possession** of the ball. Brazilian teams, however, love to entertain and score goals.

Clodoaldo took control of the ball from a teammate near the halfway line and breezed past four Italians. He passed the ball out to the left to Tostao. Tostao played a long pass directly to Jairzinho. Picking the ball up wide on the left of the pitch, Jairzinho began running at the Italian defence. He passed the ball to Pelé a few yards outside the penalty area.

Effortlessly, Pelé rolled the ball to his right, just inside the **opponents'** penalty area. Carlos Alberto had moved forward from his defensive position. Without breaking stride he smashed the ball into the goal. It flew past the Italian goalkeeper who had no chance of stopping it. It was a fantastic team goal and a fitting end to a great match.

Carlos Alberto celebrates his goal for Brazil in their 4–1 win over Italy.

PENALTY HEARTACHES

After the group stages of the **FIFA** World Cup, **penalty shoot-outs** are used to decide the winner of a match that has ended in a draw. After the standard 90 minutes of play, if the score is level, 30 minutes of **extra time** are played. If the score is still level after that, a penalty shoot-out is used. Each team has five **penalties** and the winners are the team that ends the shoot-out with the most goals. After five penalties each, if it is still a draw, then "sudden death" penalties are taken. Sudden death penalties mean that both teams take it in turns to take penalties until one of the teams miss and the other team score, winning the match.

Many famous World Cup matches have been won or lost using a penalty shoot-out. This can be an agonizing way of leaving a **tournament** for players and supporters if their team loses.

A saved penalty can be the difference between winning or losing a match. Holland's goalkeeper, Van Der Sar, has just saved this penalty.

France vs Brazil 1986 quarter-final

In this quarter-final match the score at the end of extra time was 1–1. Brazil were expected to win the match and were the favourites for the World Cup. Socrates, one of Brazil's greatest ever players, took Brazil's first penalty. His penalty was saved by the French goalkeeper Joel Bats. Bats had also saved a penalty during the match. Both teams scored their next three penalties. Michel Platini, of France, missed the target completely when it came to his turn. The score in the shoot-out was 3–3.

Michel Platini was devastated after missing his penalty against Brazil.

Julio Cesar took Brazil's fifth penalty but his effort hit the post and bounced away from the goal. Luis Fernandez had the chance to win the match for France. He coolly placed his shot into the corner of the net. France had knocked out the World Cup favourites.

West Germany vs England 1990 semi-final

This semi-final match was the furthest England had reached at a World Cup since they won the trophy in 1966. West Germany had not won the World Cup since 1974.

An entertaining match ended 1–1 after **extra time**. Both teams scored their first three **penalties**. When Stuart Pearce stepped up to take England's fourth penalty, his team were very close to appearing in their second ever World Cup final. Unfortunately for England, the West German goalkeeper Bodo Illgner guessed which way to go.

West Germany's goalkeeper, Bodo Illgner, used his legs to save Stuart Pearce's powerfully struck penalty.

West Germany took advantage and scored their next penalty. This meant England had to score their last penalty. Chris Waddle stepped up. He had to score his penalty to keep England in the match. The pressure showed as he shot his penalty wildly over the crossbar.

Brazil vs Italy 1994 final

The 1994 World Cup final was played between two of the most successful teams in the history of the **tournament**. Brazil had last won the trophy in 1970. Italy had last won the tournament in 1982.

Neither Brazil nor Italy had managed to score during the match or in extra time. The only way to separate them would be a **penalty shoot-out**. Italy had the worst possible start. Franco Baresi missed the target with his penalty. Brazil could not take advantage. Marcio Santos's penalty was saved. Both teams scored their next two penalties. Italy's next penalty was saved by Brazil's goalkeeper, Taffarel. Brazil scored their next penalty.

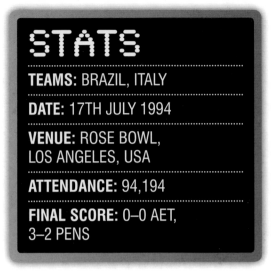

STATS

TEAMS: BRAZIL, ITALY

DATE: 17TH JULY 1994

VENUE: ROSE BOWL, LOS ANGELES, USA

ATTENDANCE: 94,194

FINAL SCORE: 0–0 AET, 3–2 PENS

The score was 3–2 when Italy's Roberto Baggio stepped up. Most **spectators** expected him to score easily from the penalty spot. Baggio blazed his shot over the crossbar. The Brazilians began to celebrate.

Roberto Baggio's penalty flew over the goal and missed. This meant that Brazil had won their fourth World Cup.

WORLD CUP MADNESS

The **FIFA** World Cup is very popular with fans all around the world. The **tournament** offers people a chance to watch great players, teams, matches, and goals. Sometimes fans also get to see moments of madness.

Diego Maradona's "Hand of God"

Diego Maradona is one of the greatest players to have played in the World Cup. He had amazing **dribbling** skills. He also had fantastic balance and vision on the pitch.

During the 1986 World Cup in Mexico Diego Maradona scored an amazing goal (see page 20). In the same match against England he also scored a goal that should not have been allowed. He used his hand to punch the ball into the goal. If you are not the goalkeeper you cannot use your hands to move the ball if you are on the pitch. The referee did not see what happened and the goal was allowed. England lost the match 2–1.

The England players and fans were angry. They could not believe the decision to allow the goal. When he was asked about what happened, Maradona said that he was proud to have scored a goal this way. He called it the "Hand of God". Argentina went on to win the World Cup in 1986. Maradona was named player of the tournament.

Zinedine Zidane's head butt

It was the 2006 World Cup final in Germany. France's captain and their most important player, Zinedine Zidane was trying to help his team beat Italy.

In **extra time** Italy **defender** Marco Materazzi appeared to say
something to Zidane. Zidane reacted by suddenly head butting
Materazzi hard in the chest. Materazzi fell to the ground. The referee
had no option but to send off Zidane. It was his last ever appearance at
the World Cup. It was also his last appearance for France. France had
to play the last few minutes of the match with only ten players. They
held out for **penalties**, but lost to Italy in the **penalty shoot-out**.

Italy's Marco Materazzi
fell to the ground after
being head butted by
France's Zinedine Zidane.

World Cup tournaments

Year	Host	Winner	Runner-up	Score
1930	Uruguay	Uruguay	Argentina	4–2
1934	Italy	Italy	Czechoslovakia	2–1 AET
1938	France	Italy	Hungary	4–2
1950	Brazil	Uruguay	Brazil	2–1
1954	Switzerland	West Germany	Hungary	3–2
1958	Sweden	Brazil	Sweden	5–2
1962	Chile	Brazil	Czechoslovakia	3–1
1966	England	England	West Germany	4–2 AET
1970	Mexico	Brazil	Italy	4–1
1974	West Germany	West Germany	Holland	2–1
1978	Argentina	Argentina	Holland	3–1 AET
1982	Spain	Italy	West Germany	3–1
1986	Mexico	Argentina	West Germany	3–2
1990	Italy	West Germany	Argentina	1–0
1994	USA	Brazil	Italy	(0–0 AET) 3–2 PENS
1998	France	France	Brazil	3–0
2002	S. Korea/Japan	Brazil	Germany	2–0
2006	Germany	Italy	France	(1–1 AET) 5–3 PENS

World Cup records

World Cup appearances

The record for the most World Cup appearances is held by Germany's Lothar Matthaus. He has played in 25 World Cup matches.

World Cup goals

Brazil's Ronaldo holds the record for the most goals scored in World Cup history. He has scored 15 goals. The record for the most goals scored in one **tournament** is held by France's Just Fontaine. He scored an amazing 13 goals in 1958.

The fastest goal

The fastest goal ever scored in a World Cup match was scored by Turkey's Hakan Suker against South Korea in 2002. It took only 11 seconds for Sukur to score!

Red card record

The World Cup record that no player wants is the one for the quickest red card in World Cup history. This record is held by Uruguay's Jose Batista, who was sent off against Scotland in 1986 after only 56 seconds!

Highest attendance

The highest attendance in World Cup history is 174,000. This record was set in 1950 when Brazil played Uruguay in the World Cup final at the Maracana Stadium in Rio de Janeiro, Brazil.

Books to read

David Beckham: My Side, David Beckham (HarperCollinsWillow, 2004)

Essential Sports: Football, (2nd Edition), Andy Smith (Heinemann Library, 2008)

Football: The Ultimate Guide (Dorling Kindersley Publishers Ltd, 2008)

Sport Files: Wayne Rooney, John Townsend (Raintree, 2008)

The Usborne Little Book of Soccer Skills (Usborne Publishing Ltd, 2005)

World Football Stars (Top Trumps), Nick Judd and Tim Dykes (JH Haynes & Co Ltd, 2007)

Websites

www.fifa.com
This website has all of the information about the FIFA World Cup. It is great for finding out about your favourite players and teams.

http://news.bbc.co.uk/sport1/football
You can keep up to date with all the latest football news and match results at the BBC Sports news pages.

GLOSSARY

continent one of the world's largest land masses. Continents are usually divided into many countries. There are seven continents on Earth.

controversy argument or difference of opinion

defender position of a footballer on the pitch. Defenders try to stop the opposition from scoring.

dribble run with the ball at your feet

extra time extra period of play that is added on to a football match if it is a draw at the end of normal time (90 minutes). Extra time lasts for 30 minutes, with two halves of 15 minutes each.

FIFA (*Fédération International de Football Association*) the international organization responsible for football around the world

free kick kick of the ball awarded by the referee after a foul

host team holding an event in their own country

incisive quick and skilful passing of the ball

inferior less successful than. An inferior team will have won fewer tournaments than a superior, more successful one.

legend extremely famous person who is well-known for their particular talent or success

midfielder player or players positioned in the middle of the pitch who link the attacking and defending players

opponent person or team that you are playing against

penalty the referee gives a penalty if a foul happens in the 18-yard box. The ball is placed on a spot 12 yards from the goal and only the goalkeeper is allowed to stop the shot.

penalty shoot-out after extra time, if the scores are still level, the two teams pick five players from each team to try and score five penalties. The team that scores the most penalties wins.

political tension unease and disagreement between two countries

possession keeping the ball with your team. If a team keeps possession of the ball then the opposition cannot score.

spectator person watching a match

tactics way in which a team plans to play, agreed between the players and their manager

technique way of doing something. Different players control the ball in different ways on the football pitch, and there is good and bad technique for certain passes and skills.

through-ball pass beyond the opposition defence that creates a goal-scoring opportunity

tournament organized number of matches that lead to a final. The winner of the final game wins the tournament.

INDEX